THIS BOOK
BELONGS TO

. . . .

. . . .

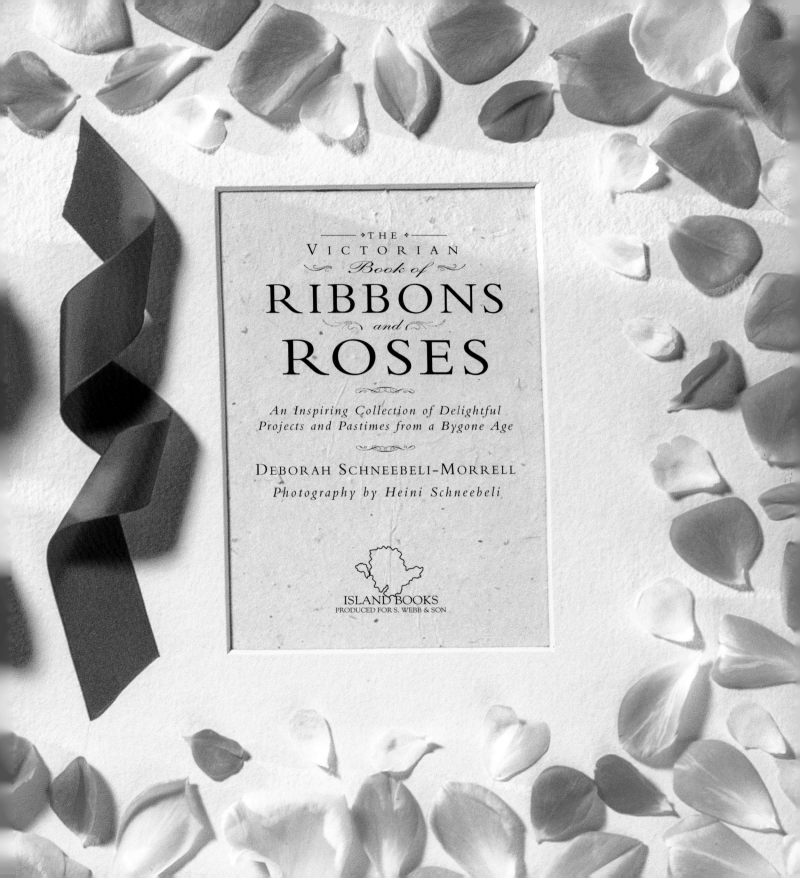

THE
VICTORIAN
Book of
RIBBONS
and
ROSES

An Inspiring Collection of Delightful
Projects and Pastimes from a Bygone Age

D E B O R A H   S C H N E E B E L I - M O R R E L L

Photography by Heini Schneebeli

ISLAND BOOKS
PRODUCED FOR S. WEBB & SON

The Victorian Book of
Ribbons and Roses

Designed and created by
THE BRIDGEWATER BOOK COMPANY LTD

Art Director: Peter Bridgewater
Designer: Jane Lanaway
Editor: Geraldine Christy
Managing Editor: Mandy Greenfield
Photography: Heini Schneebeli
Page make-up: Chris Lanaway

CLB 4088

This edition published by S. Webb & Son

© 1995 CLB Publishing
Godalming, Surrey

Colour separation by HBM Print Ltd, Singapore
Printed and bound in Singapore by Tien Wah Press
ISBN 1-85833-502-7

CONTENTS

INTRODUCTION

❦

*T*HERE WAS a flowering of domestic creativity in the Victorian era, generally in the domain of middle-class ladies. New developments in the printing industry gave rise to the publishing of an abundance of ladies' magazines and books, which offered advice on household matters as well as inspiration, templates and patterns for all manner of fancy work, stitching and needlecrafts. Today you can see examples of these drawing-room skills by visiting museums and antique fairs; indeed, you may have inherited one or two items, some sewing equipment, or a scrapbook or decorated photograph album.

The projects in this book are inspired by the spirit and visual aesthetics of the nineteenth century, and aim to evoke the atmosphere of a more tranquil time. The practical little découpaged letter rack on page 17 and the delightful Valentines on pages 28–9, made out of cut, shaped and pinked-edged paper, Victorian scraps and ribbon bows, are examples of traditional work, while the ribbon-decorated combs on pages 24–5 have been directly inspired by patterns seen in ladies' fashion magazines. Modern methods have also been used, and although the book plate on pages 14–15 looks authentic, it has actually been achieved with the aid of photocopying – a technique that the Victorians surely would have appreciated!

The Victorians loved flowers and much favoured the rose, which has inspired love poetry throughout the ages and was the subject of much sentimental verse composed by amateur authors. Gardening was another favourite Victorian pastime and roses were widely cultivated. Buds and flowers were collected, dried and preserved in the form of faded papery arrangements, which were often displayed under a glass dome; refreshing rosewater tonics were made; and fragrant pot pourris, as shown on pages 12–13, were sometimes made into charming little rose-scented sachets, like those on page 33, and then slipped between fresh laundry.

Queen Victoria's passion for Scotland inspired a craze for using tartan. The picture frames on pages 36–7 have been cleverly decorated with pretty tartan ribbons. Ribbon work was very popular, used extensively to trim and decorate clothes and hats. The sewing basket quilt on pages 40–1, although not strictly traditional in style, uses beautiful Victorian feather-edged chequered ribbon with pearl buttons to stunning effect.

Beautiful richly patterned and coloured ribbons are now much easier to find and there are specialist shops that carry reproductions of old designs. An extraordinary variety of style, colour and fabric is available, and even the names of ribbons are inspiring – silks, satins, sheers, moiré, velvets, taffetas, chiffon, wire-edged and feather-dyed. There is an endless list of ribbons to enjoy and use creatively.

ROSE POT POURRI

$\mathcal{U}$SED THROUGHOUT history, no scent is more evocative of a summer garden than the rich, heady perfume of a rose, the most traditional ingredient of all pot pourri recipes. It was in the eighteenth century that the term pot pourri came to mean a fragrant mixture of herbs, flowers and spices used to decorate and perfume houses. A well-appointed Victorian home had pretty bowls or baskets of highly scented and home-prepared pot pourri displayed in all the important rooms. There is nothing to surpass the wonderful faded, papery quality of dried rose blooms; use a subtle mixture of reds, pinks and scarlets laced with oakmoss, or combine your colours to create a more vibrant or busy mixture.

MATERIALS

1 tablespoon ground cinnamon

30 g (1¼ oz) orris root powder

7 drops of rose essential oil

3 drops of cottage garden mixture essential oil

1 vanilla pod

1 litre (2 pt) mixed dried rose petals, buds and blooms

25 g (1 oz) oakmoss

25 g (1 oz) lavender

25 g (1 oz) lemon verbena

Small handful of whole cloves

1 In a small bowl mix together the cinnamon, orris root powder and essential oils.

2 Rub the mixture between your fingers, making sure that the oil penetrates the mixture evenly.

3 Cut and split the vanilla pod into small pieces and mix together with all the remaining ingredients in a large bowl. Remember to put aside some oakmoss, rosebuds, blooms and petals for the surface decoration.

4 Add the mixture of fixative (orris root), spices and oils to the bowl of dry ingredients. Stir together to produce an evenly scented mixture.

5 Put the mixture in an airtight container and place it in the dark for three weeks, occasionally shaking the container. The longer you leave the mixture, the stronger the fragrance will become. Eventually remove it from the airtight container and display in a favourite bowl.

BOOKMARK

*B*OOKS IN THE Victorian household were treasured possessions. They usually had marbled endpapers and it was common for the owner of the book to paste a personal decorated book plate at the beginning. Bookmarks were often of embossed leather, but a silk or satin ribbon or tasselled braid was a more appropriate marker for a book of sentimental poetry. This sumptuous gold and black braid and tasselled bookmark is simplicity itself to make.

MATERIALS

22 cm (9 in) of ornate gold and black braid 4 cm (1½ in) wide

Fabric glue

Gold tassel

1 Fold over the top end of the braid and fix it with fabric glue. Do not use too much glue or it may be visible from the front of the bookmark. It may be necessary to hold the braid until the glue is firmly set.

2 Turn over 2 cm (¾ in) at the other end of the braid. Before gluing in place, make a small hole in the centre along the fold.

3 Thread the tassel cord through this hole, spread a small amount of glue under the folded hem and press firmly until the glue has set.

4 Turn the two corners over at 45-degree angles to make a pointed edge where the braid meets the tassels. Glue and hold until set.

BOOK PLATE

*W*ith the use of photocopying it is so easy to make a collection of personalized book plates. The one shown here has been hand coloured and 'antiqued' by painting with a weak coat of black tea.

MATERIALS

Selection of black and white engravings of borders, flower basket and lettering

White paper

Spray mount adhesive or paper paste

Weak tea

Coloured pencils

1 Select an appealing black and white engraving; a basket of roses has been chosen here. Cut it out and paste it onto white paper.

2 Cut out a border to frame the basket of roses. Remember to leave enough space below for the lettering and name to be inscribed. Mitre the corners carefully and stick down.

3 Cut out, assemble and place Ex Libris letters in position. If you have access to a word processor it is very easy to design and print this type. Photocopy the image several times. It is at this stage that you may want to enlarge or reduce the size of your image.

4 Paint the book plate with tea, and allow to dry. If the paper crinkles slightly, iron it flat with a medium hot iron. Hand-colour the basket of flowers and frame with coloured pencils and paste the finished book plate into your favourite book.

Elphinston: *What, have you not read it through?*
Johnson: *No Sir, do you read books through?*

SAMUEL JOHNSON 1709–84

*Each book that a young girl touches should be
bound in white vellum.*

JOHN RUSKIN 1819–1900

LOVE LETTERS

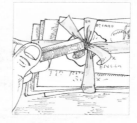

> My Darling, be a wife, be a friend, write good
> letters, do not mope, do not torment me.
>
> ANTON CHEKHOV 1860–1904

1 *Tie the ribbon around the bundle of letters as shown, and knot at the top.*

2 *Put a piece of aluminium foil under the knot to protect the letters from the heat of the wax. Light the wick of the sealing wax and drip the hot wax carefully onto the knot.*

*T*HE ART OF letter writing was much practised by the Victorians and most people were expected to write a beautiful hand. The introduction of the penny post in the early 1840s made the sending of letters altogether much simpler, and affectionate letters were exchanged between women friends. Love letters needed to be kept secure, however, and what prettier way than by tying with a faded pink satin ribbon and sealing the contents from prying eyes with sealing wax?

MATERIALS

1 m (3¼ ft) faded pink satin ribbon

Small piece of aluminium foil

Stick of blue sealing wax

Matches

Coin or embossed head of upholstery tack

3 *Working quickly, before the wax cools down, press the embossed surface of the coin or upholstery tack onto the warm wax to make an impression.*

4 *Cut the ends of the ribbon at an angle as shown.*

LETTER RACK

*T*HIS DELIGHTFUL and practical découpage letter rack is just the thing to grace your writing desk. Letter racks made from wood or strong card are available ready-made from most good stationery shops or are easy to assemble from craft suppliers. Gift wrapping paper, made from Victorian facsimile wallpaper designs, has been used along with a crackle varnish to give the letter rack an authentic feel.

*I*t may sound like being over particular, but we recommend persons to make a practice of fully addressing notes etc., on all occasions.

Enquire Within Upon Everything 1894

MATERIALS

Wooden or cardboard letter rack

Victorian-style wrapping paper

Scissors

Wallpaper paste

PVA glue

Crackle glaze stages 1 and 2

Paintbrush for glaze

Raw umber oil paint

Rag

Polyurethane matt-finish varnish

Paintbrush for varnish

Fine sandpaper

1 Cut the paper into pieces slightly larger than each side to be covered. Start with the centre panel. Snip along the curved edge of the paper to be applied to the three curved panels.

2 Mix the wallpaper paste and apply to the surface of the letter rack. Carefully smooth the paper onto the central panel front, taking care to smooth out any bubbles with your fingers. Turn over the snipped edge and paste firmly to the back of the panel. Cover the back with a piece slightly shorter and cut into a curve to hide the snipped 'turn over'.

3 Repeat this process with the front and back panels and continue to paper all sides inside and out. Allow to dry, then cover the base in the same way and stick to the bottom of the letter rack with PVA glue.

4 Apply the crackle glaze in two stages, following the manufacturer's instructions. After the second coat, when the glaze has crackled, rub a small quantity of raw umber oil pigment into the cracks. Rub off the excess and allow to dry.

5 Varnish with three coats of polyurethane varnish and sand the penultimate coat lightly before applying the final finishing coat.

DÉCOUPAGE BOX

DÉCOUPAGE, a craft with a long history, became a very
fashionable occupation in the nineteenth century. Technical developments
in printing made it possible for everybody to collect great varieties of
printed and embossed colours, images and scraps. These were avidly
swapped between friends and pasted into albums and onto boxes, screens,
trunks, frames and book covers, as well as having many other applications.
Victorian scraps are still available today and it is relatively easy to find a
choice of shapes and sizes of blank wooden or card boxes to decorate.

MATERIALS

Hexagonal box

Green paint

Paint brush

Victorian scraps – bride, roses and butterflies

Scissors

Wallpaper paste

Paste brush

Sheet of orange or pink recycled paper

Pinking shears

Polyurethane satin-finish varnish

Paintbrush for varnish

Fine sandpaper

He had 42 boxes, all carefully packed,
With his name painted clearly on each
But, since he omitted to mention the fact,
They were all left behind on the beach.

The Hunting of the Snark
LEWIS CARROLL 1832–98

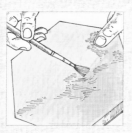 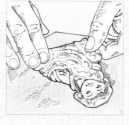   

1 Give the box and lid two coats of green paint. Allow to dry.

2 Cut out the scraps carefully and lay them onto the lid of the box to plan your design. Remove, then paste the surface of the lid and stick the first scrap in place.

3 Paste the roses to one side of the figure and the butterflies to the other.

4 Cut a strip of the orange or pink paper 2 cm (¾ in) wide. Make a zigzag edge on one side with the pinking shears and cut a scalloped edge on the other with ordinary scissors. Paste around the edge of the lid, overlapping the side.

5 Add more 'pinked' paper strips to decorate around the base of the lid and the bottom of the box. When thoroughly dry, varnish with three coats of polyurethane varnish, sanding the penultimate coat to achieve a smooth finish.

PAINTED BOXES

Any one of this appealing assortment of decorated boxes would make a lovely gift, perhaps containing homemade sweets or jewels, a shell collection, ribbons, or sewing equipment. Or you could fill a rose-adorned, heart-shaped, beribboned box with deliciously scented pot pourri. Here is how to make a painted box with combed paint decoration.

MATERIALS

Oval box

Cream paint

Dark blue paint

Decorator's rubber comb

Paintbrush with a pointed end to its handle

Polyurethane satin-finish varnish

Paintbrush for varnish

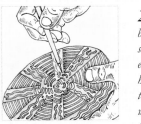

2 Scratch squiggles in between the combed sections with the sharp end of the paintbrush handle. Allow the paint to dry and varnish with three coats of polyurethane varnish.

1 Paint the box with two coats of cream paint. Allow to dry. Paint on the blue paint and, while it is still wet, comb the pattern into the paint, revealing the cream paint underneath.

DECORATIVE KEYS

*T*HE HOUSEKEEPER, as head of the Victorian household, carried her symbol of office, the châtelaine, hung with the keys to the still room, linen and store cupboards, about her waist. The jangling of the keys warned any inattentive underservants of her approach. Beautiful tassels are surprisingly easy to make in many different threads, shapes and sizes and they look very effective when attached to a special key, perhaps for a writing desk, linen cupboard or jewel box.

MATERIALS

1 skein each of green and orange cotton twist embroidery thread

Small amount of cotton wool

Needle

40 cm (16 in) gold cord

The key of India is in London.
BENJAMIN DISRAELI
House of Lords
5 MARCH 1881

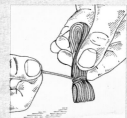

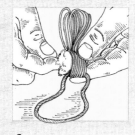

1 *Wind the green and orange thread a number of times around your fingers held flat. The more times you wind, the thicker the tassel will be.*

2 *Slide the thread from your fingers and wind some orange thread around the tassel one-third of the way down; tuck in the end.*

3 *To enlarge the size of the head, push some cotton wool wadding in with a blunt needle. Stuff the head evenly and bring the thread around the cotton wool to hide it. Insert the cord at this stage, hiding the join in the head.*

4 *Thread some orange thread and work blanket stitch all around the head, working each row into the previous row. Decrease the number of stitches as you reach the top. Finish and push the needle through the tassel to finish.*

5 *Knot the cord close to the head of the tassel and, finally, trim the loops at the base of the tassel so that the ends are even.*

DÉCOUPAGE KEY FOB

*F*OR LESS SPECIAL, but equally important, keys a lovely découpage key fob is ideal. These are quick to make from thin plywood and are commonly available from craft shops and hardware stores. They can be decorated with a variety of pretty Victorian scraps.

MATERIALS

Wooden key fobs

Fine sandpaper

Terracotta paint

Paintbrush

Victorian scraps of flowers

Scissors

Wallpaper paste

Paste brush

Polyurethane satin-finish varnish

Paintbrush for varnish

'There's an accident' they said. 'Your servant's cut in half, he's dead!' 'Indeed!' said Mr Jones, 'and please Send me the half that's got my keys.'

Ruthless Rhymes for Heartless Homes
HARRY GRAHAM
1874–1936

1 *Lightly sand the fob to make a smooth surface. Paint the fob with two coats of paint. Allow to dry.*

A golden key can open any door.
English Proverb

2 *Cut out your scraps carefully. Paste the surface of the fob and press each scrap firmly down in the centre, smoothing with your fingers to ensure no air bubbles are trapped. Allow to dry thoroughly.*

3 *Varnish with at least three coats of polyurethane varnish to protect. If you want a more antique look, tint the varnish with a minute quantity of raw umber oil paint.*

ROSEBUD HEART

DURING LONG cold winters when it was nearly impossible to find fresh flowers, the Victorians arranged garden flowers that had been picked and dried in the summer months to make lovely floral displays. Dried roses and rosebuds are available from good florists or you can pick and dry them yourself. These charming little rosebud hearts can be scented with rose oil and hung in the linen cupboard to impart their heady fragrance, which is so evocative of an English garden.

MATERIALS

Approximately 25 tiny pink closed rosebuds

5 slightly more open deeper pink buds

Rose essential oil

50 cm (20 in) flexible wire (garden wire is ideal)

Pliers (long-nosed)

Two 50 cm (20 in) lengths of light and dark pink chiffon ribbon

*... be but sworn my love, and
I'll no longer be a Capulet ...
What's in a name? That which we call a rose
By any other name would smell as sweet.*

Romeo and Juliet
WILLIAM SHAKESPEARE
1564–1616

1 *Put all the rosebuds in a small bowl and sprinkle 7 drops of rose oil onto them.*

2 *Bend the wire into a heart shape, so that the ends of the wire meet at the top of the heart.*

3 *Begin to thread the rosebuds onto one half of the heart by pushing the end of the wire gently through the thicker base of each bud. After every four or five tiny buds, thread on a larger one. Complete one side of the heart.*

4 *Now thread a symmetrical number of buds onto the other side of the heart. Join the wire firmly at the top with the pliers.*

5 *Tie the double ribbon over the wire join and arrange all the buds so that their bases face into the heart and the tips of the buds are visible from the front of the heart.*

ROSETTE

*W*ith a needle and thread gather together a 15 cm (6 in) length of delicate lace into a rosette. Sew into the centre of the heart over the wire join. For a pretty finishing touch, attach a tiny rosebud to the middle of the rosette. Hang the heart as decoration on a bedroom or dressing-room wall or slip over the wire handle of a coat-hanger that holds your favourite outfit.

HAIR COMBS

$\mathcal{F}$ASHION WAS followed with great diligence in Victorian times. Combs, ribbons, lace and hats were carefully chosen to match and complement the day's outfit. These beautiful ribbon-adorned hair combs are directly inspired by some examples from Victorian ladies' fashion magazines.

MATERIALS

1 flat-topped button approximately 2.5 cm (1 in) wide

30 cm (12 in) of rainbow-dyed wire-edged ribbon 4 cm (1½ in) wide

Needle

Thread

85 cm (34 in) of dip-dyed burnt orange ribbon 4 cm (1½ in) wide

40 cm (16 in) of shot silk orange ribbon 5 cm (2 in) wide

Hair comb with two long prongs

Florist's wire

1 Lay the button onto a 4 cm (1½ in) length of rainbow ribbon. With the needle and thread, gather the ribbon edges together at the back of the button and finish off tightly.

2 Gather the remaining rainbow ribbon into a rosette by securing one end and pulling the fine wire along the edge. Sew a seam at the join. Sew the button onto the rosette.

*O*nce you have made this simple ribbon decoration, try using contrasting combinations of patterned and plain ribbons. Use bows and pompoms or, for a really extravagant design, try including brightly coloured feathers.

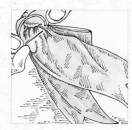

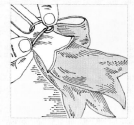

3 Fold the dip-dyed burnt orange ribbon into three loops. The middle loop, placed behind the other two loops, needs to be 3 cm (1¼ in) longer. Sew in place behind the rosette.

4 Fold the shot silk ribbon in half and sew it behind the previous three loops, with the ends slightly apart. Cut V shapes to finish off the ribbon ends.

5 The ribbon decoration may now be sewn onto the comb, if the comb has conveniently placed holes to sew through. If not, it is probably easier to fix with soft fine florist's wire.

6 Take the wire between the two short folds and one long fold of burnt orange ribbon and wind three times around the top of the comb. Twist to secure and then tuck the wire ends out of sight.

Only God, my dear, Could love you for yourself alone And not your yellow hair.

Oedipus at Colonus
W. B. YEATS
1865–1939

EASTER EGGS

*T*HE EGG IS a potent symbol of creation and the decoration of eggs at Easter has become a universal Christian tradition. In Central Europe real eggs are stunningly decorated in a number of ways; they are etched, batiked, engraved, painted or beaded, each one bearing the individuality of its maker.

MATERIALS

Papier mâché Easter egg case
Collection of glittering sweet wrappers
Scissors
PVA glue, very slightly diluted
Small paintbrush
1 m (3¼ ft) of gold ribbon 2.5 cm (1 in) wide
1 m (3¼ ft) of gold ribbon 1 cm (½ in) wide

*T*he papier mâché egg cases used here are easy to obtain. Here one has been découpaged with a crazy patchwork of glittering sweet wrappers and tied together with a sumptuous gold bow to enclose its enticing contents.

*W*hen love
is declared on
Easter Day
A marriage is certain
the following May.

English
Proverb

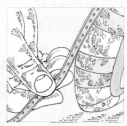

1 *Cut the glittery papers into even-sized strips slightly wider at one end. They do not need to be long enough to reach the centre of the egg. Decide how you are going to place them around the egg, contrasting the colour and pattern for maximum effect.*

2 *Start on one side of the egg. Paint the area to be covered with PVA glue and press the glittery paper in place; turn the paper strip over the rim of the egg and stick down just inside. Continue around the egg, alternating the colours. Press down firmly to eliminate any folds or creases.*

3 *Stick some more paper in a crazy patchwork fashion into an oval shape in the centre of the egg case and enclose it with a band of wide gold ribbon. Allow to dry. Decorate the other half of the egg in the same manner.*

4 *Stick the thinner gold ribbon in a band around the rim on each side of the egg. Pack with delicious Easter treats and tie with a beautiful shimmering gold bow.*

The practice of giving chocolate eggs as presents at Easter was introduced to England from Germany, as were so many charming customs, during the nineteenth century. At this time exquisite papier mâché egg 'cases' were widely sold. Most often they were découpaged with Easter subjects, the Easter rabbit being a favourite motif. The cases were filled with an assortment of chocolate eggs and given as presents to children on Easter Sunday.

VALENTINES CARDS

*I*N VICTORIAN TIMES most homes would have had a copy of *The Language of Flowers*, a much prized and useful little book. It was an index of the symbolic meaning of hundreds of flowers. This popular book was widely interpreted, and both fresh flowers and images of flowers, as used in Valentines, carried specific symbolic meanings. Of the flowers most commonly used to convey messages between lovers:

A rose meant 'love'
A pansy meant 'thought'
Lily of the valley meant 'a return to happiness'.

MATERIALS

Gold doily	Small pointed scissors
Large scissors	Paler pink stiff paper
Paper glue	12 pink sequins
Dark pink card	Craft knife
Pinking shears	Approximately 1 m (3¼ ft) gold ribbon
Victorian embossed scraps of flowers	Pink paper lace

1 Cut out a ring from the centre of the gold doily. With the paper glue, stick this ring onto a slightly larger circle of the dark pink card. Cut around this circle with the pinking shears to make a zigzagged edge.

2 Cut out the scrap carefully with the small pointed scissors. Stick carefully onto the centre of the circle. Now stick this circle onto a 14 cm (5¼ in) square of paler pink paper. Stick 12 sequins in place around the central motif.

3 Cut, with the craft knife, two ribbon-width slits between each sequin. Thread the gold ribbon behind the sequins and through the slits; tie into a bow at the top of the card. Make a border by sticking lengths of paper lace around the outside of the pink square.

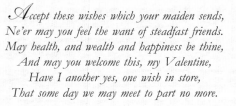

Accept these wishes which your maiden sends,
Ne'er may you feel the want of steadfast friends.
May health, and wealth and happiness be thine,
And may you welcome this, my Valentine,
Have I another yes, one wish in store,
That some day we may meet to part no more.

VALENTINE C.1840

VALENTINE VERSE

❧ ❧

Will you, won't you,
Do you, don't you
Love me, Darling Valentine?
For I love you very dearly,
And I want you to be mine.

The music of your voice
Just makes my heart rejoice,
For I know that
You are mine.
My own sweet Valentine.

A feast of flowers here behold
A thing of joy to see
But Ah! to me 'tis sweeter far
To feast mine eyes on thee.

VICTORIAN VALENTINE VERSE
ANON

❧ ❧

ROSES AND ORANGES

THIS RICHLY opulent pyramid of alternate layers of tiny kumquats and rich red dried roses will stun and delight guests. Place the pyramid in the centre of the dining table for special occasions or perhaps among the delicious desserts waiting to be served from the chiffonier or sideboard.

1 Break off the stems, leaving 2 cm (³⁄4 in) on all the dried flowers.

2 Place the oasis cone in the creamware dish. Gently, but firmly, push a row of peonies around the base of the cone.

3 Cut lengths of florist's wire approximately 10 cm (4 in) long. Push the wires through the end of the kumquats, then fold the ends of the wires together and push into the oasis to fix the kumquats in a tight row above the peonies.

MATERIALS

Bunches of dried African marigolds, deep red and vermilion roses and pink peonies

Creamware stemmed bowl

Oasis cone 25 cm (10 in) high

Stiff florist's wire

1 lb (500 g) fresh kumquats

My love is like a red red rose
That's newly sprung in June
My love is like the melody
That's sweetly play'd in tune.

A Selection of Scots Songs II 1794
ROBERT BURNS 1759–96

4 Add a layer of vermilion roses, followed by a row of marigolds and peonies, then another row of deep red roses.

5 Add a second row of kumquats and then continue building up alternate layers of the different flowers.

6 Nearer the top of the pyramid you will need to slice off the ends of the kumquats, before you thread the wire through, so that they do not stand proud of the flowers.

7 Continue with alternate layers and top with a single kumquat.

POMANDERS

$\mathcal{T}$HESE CHARMING variations of the more well-known
clove-spiced orange pomanders are quick and simple to make.
They look their best piled together in a pretty china bowl. A delicious
mingling of perfumed and spicy scents has been achieved by laying
the pomanders on a fragrant bed of whole cloves.

*1 Push the tiny pink
rosebuds one by one into
the oasis ball, making
sure they are tightly
packed together and no
oasis is visible between
the buds.*

*2 Continue adding
buds and, at regularly
spaced intervals, push
in a single more open,
deeper-coloured rosebud.*

*3 Continue in this
manner all around
the ball until it is
evenly covered.*

*4 When the ball is
completely covered,
sprinkle a few drops
of rose oil over the
pomander.*

MATERIALS

*Oasis balls of varying sizes,
the largest 10 cm (4 in)
in diameter*

*Large number of tiny
pink rosebuds (usually
sold by weight)*

*Smaller number of deep red,
yellow and deep pink
half-opened rosebuds*

Rose essential oil

$\mathcal{T}$ry arranging different
coloured rosebuds into
patterns around the
oasis ball, or use in
combination with other
dried garden flowers.

ROSE SACHETS

$\mathcal{T}$HESE DELIGHTFUL little rose-scented sachets will gently impart their subtle fragrance to your fresh laundry when slipped between clothes in a chest of drawers. On the square sachet, the central rose motif has been cleverly framed by a circlet of lace.

MATERIALS

3 lengths of 20 cm (8 in) of fine cotton, each printed with a different rose design

Needle

Thread

Rose-scented pot pourri

A variety of lace for edging, approximately 60 cm (2 ft) for each sachet

Grey wire-edged, faded pink satin and fuchsia pink silk ribbons for bows to decorate

1 *Cut 2 identical pieces in each cotton of a circle, square and diamond shape. All should be no more than 10 cm (4 in) wide.*

2 *Turn the right sides together and hand or machine stitch around the edge, leaving a 4 cm (1½ in) un-sewn gap.*

3 *Turn the sachets the right way out and lightly fill them with the pot pourri. Sew the gap in the seam neatly.*

4 *Neatly sew the lace around the sachets by hand, taking care at the corners. You will need to gather the lace around the round sachet. For the finishing touch, sew on small tightly tied bows.*

LAMPSHADE

Until the 1880s homes were lit either by dim gas lights, candles or traditional oil lamps. It was then that the wonderfully bright incandescent gas mantle was developed, followed shortly afterwards by what seemed to be miraculous electric light. This exciting invention prompted the most profound change in house decoration, as furniture no longer needed to be arranged and clustered around a dim light source. A new, simple and less cluttered house style emerged that went on to become the Arts and Crafts movement. This sunny daffodil-yellow lampshade has been imaginatively adorned with lace rose motifs, used for appliqué designs in dressmaking; these are commonly available in good haberdashery shops. Finishing with fringed braid gives the shade a very Victorian feel.

MATERIALS

*Small yellow fabric lampshade, 15 cm (6 in) high,
with top diameter 10 cm (4 in) and
bottom diameter 25 cm (10 in)*

4 or more (depending on size) lace rose motifs

Fabric glue

1 m (3¼ ft) off-white fringed satin braid

50 cm (20 in) matching braid for top

*Treat your friends as you do your
pictures, and place them in their best light.*

JENNIE JEROME CHURCHILL
Mother of Winston Churchill

*To prevent the Smoking of a lamp. Soak the wick
in strong vinegar, and dry it well before you use it;
the flame will then burn clear and bright.*

ENQUIRE WITHIN UPON EVERYTHING 1894

THE LAMPLIGHTER

The installation of public street lighting was a welcome introduction to life in the nineteenth century. Gas lamps were lit at dusk by the lamplighter, a popular character whose presence was a discouragement to criminals. He would extinguish the lamps at dawn accompanied by a chorus of singing birds.

1 *Arrange the lace motifs around the centre of the lampshade so that they are evenly spaced. Stick them very carefully in place onto the shade with small amounts of fabric glue (this can be easily removed if you get it in the wrong place).*

2 *Cut the fringed braid to the right length for the bottom rim, allowing a little extra to overlap in order to make a neat join. Stick along the bottom edge very evenly, making sure that the fringe hangs down beneath.*

3 *Cut the matching braid for the top edge and stick in place with the fabric glue. Pay particular attention to the join. A little extra glue here will stop the edges fraying.*

The best oil for lamps, whether animal, vegetable or mineral, is that which is clear and nearly colourless, like water.

Enquire Within Upon
Everything 1894

The last day in September – immensely cold, a kind of solid cold outside the windows … Don't read this. Do you hear that train whistle and now the leaves – the dry leaves – and now the fire-fluttering and creaking … Why doesn't she bring the lamps?

KATHERINE MANSFIELD
Hampstead 30 SEPTEMBER 1918

PICTURE FRAMES

❦

THE VICTORIAN passion for tartan was inspired by Queen Victoria's love of Scotland and all things Scottish. Souvenirs, pictures and all manner of ornaments in the Scottish style were collected and tartan was used decoratively, either painted or as printed paper, throughout the home to cover picture frames, sewing boxes, trinket boxes and many other items. It was popular with milliners and dressmakers, and tartan fabric and ribbons were often woven in the finest silk. Tartan ribbons are still popular today and these picture frames have been deftly decorated with ribbons and rosettes.

MATERIALS

*Picture frame 15 cm (6 in) square, with a
4.5 cm (1¾ in) wide flat front*

Dark green paint

Paintbrush

1 m (3¼ ft) of tartan ribbon 3.5 cm (1½ in) wide

Scissors

Double-sided adhesive tape

*80 cm (32 in) of wire-edged purple ribbon
2.5 cm (1 in) wide*

Scraps of leather

Pinking shears

4 decorative upholstery nails

Hammer

Try designing a complementary group of tartan picture frames to hang together. On the smaller frame above, narrower ribbon has been used and the corners are marked with single upholstery nails. For the larger one in the main picture, the frame has been completely covered in tartan fabric and outlined in plum-coloured braid, a real favourite of the period.

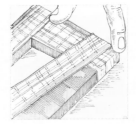

1 Paint the frame with 2 coats of dark green paint. Allow to dry between each coat.

2 Cut the tartan ribbon into four strips; it should be long enough to stretch around to the back of the frame and overlap by 2 cm (³⁄4 in). Place double-sided tape where the ribbon is to be stuck. Pull the ribbon taut and press down onto the tape, over the sides and secure it on the back of the frame. Complete all four sides in this way.

3 Cut the purple ribbon in 20 cm (8 in) lengths. Secure one end of the wire that runs through the edge and pull the other to gather the rosette. Secure the wire to hold the gathers, fold back both ends and disguise the join in the folds of the rosette.

4 Cut 4 small circles of leather 3 cm (1¹⁄4 in) in diameter with the pinking shears.

5 Place the rosettes on each corner of the frame and nail through the centre of the leather and rosette with the decorative upholstery nail.

Guard against unnecessary over-embellishment in the decoration of small frames, so as not to detract from the image therein.

SUMMER BONNET

*L*ADIES' FASHION was of the utmost importance in Victorian times and middle-class women possessed a hat for every season and for all manner of occasions. These were often decorated with a stunning variety of trimmings, ribbon bows, rosettes, feathers, braids, and even fresh flowers. This beautiful antique straw bonnet has been elegantly trimmed with a circlet of wide taffeta ribbon and an abundance of pretty wired ribbon roses. To achieve the faded cabbage-rose effect, shaded taffeta ribbon has been used, with a darker shade along one side of the ribbon.

BLEACHING STRAW BONNETS

Wash them in pure water, scrubbing them with a brush. Then put them in a box in which has been set a saucer of burning sulphur. Cover them up, so that the fumes may bleach them.

ENQUIRE WITHIN UPON EVERYTHING 1894

American ladies who wish for a kiss,
Will remove their own hat
and put on his.

MATERIALS

Straw hat with wide rim

1.5 m (4¾ ft) of wire-edged orange taffeta ribbon 4 cm (1½ in) wide

Needle

Matching thread

Scissors

1 m (3¼ ft) of wire-edged orange taffeta ribbon 7 cm (3 in) wide

A selection of wire-edged shaded taffeta ribbons in 7 colours – pinks, purples, reds and orange. Each ribbon should be 50 cm (20 in) long and 4 cm (1½ in) wide

1 m (3¼ ft) of bronze wire-edged taffeta ribbon 5 cm (2 in) wide

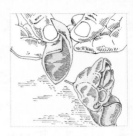

1 Bind the edge of the rim of the hat with the 4 cm (1½ in) wide orange taffeta ribbon. Very slightly gather the ribbon along the wire edges. This helps you to stitch it neatly around the curve.

2 Sew the wider orange taffeta ribbon loosely around the centre of the hat. Ruckle it slightly and hold in place with tiny, widely spaced stitches.

3 To make a ribbon rose, take a 50 cm (20 in) length of ribbon. Fasten one end of the wire that runs through the edge. Pull the ribbon along this wire and gather tightly.

4 Fold the end of the ribbon over and turn the gathered ribbon around on itself to form a flower shape. Use the drawn-up wire to bind the base of the 'rose'.

5 Make a number of rose leaves by taking a 15 cm (6 in) length of bronze ribbon. Find the middle point of one side and fold the top edge either side of this middle point down over the ribbon. Turn over and fold the edges to the middle. Stitch to close and attach to the side of the rose. Sew a group of seven leaves and roses onto the back of the hat where the ruckled ribbon splits into a tail.

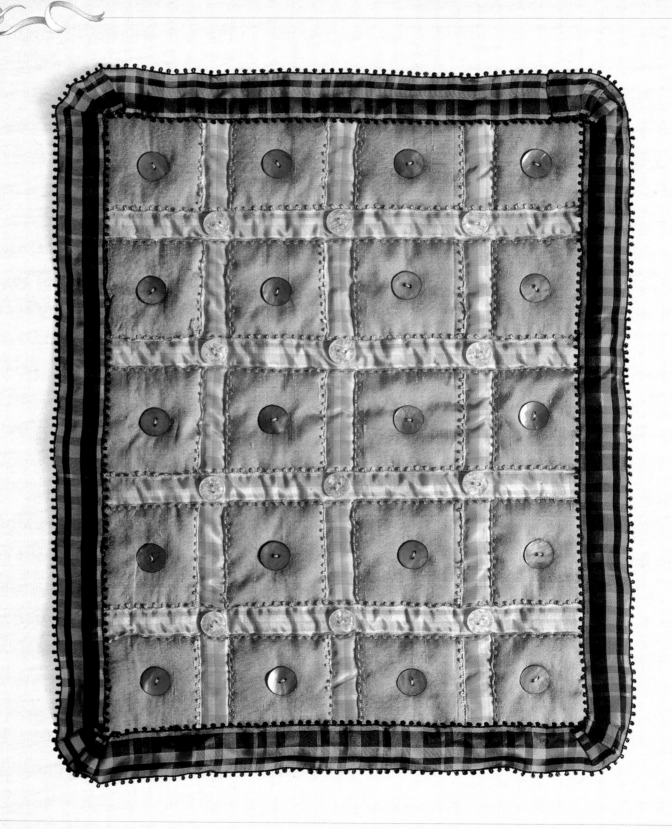

BUTTON QUILT

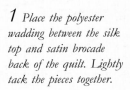

HE NEWLY rich middle-class women in the nineteenth century who could afford to employ servants found themselves with an increasing amount of leisure time. They practised all manner of needlework and sewing activities and generally achieved high levels of skill in a variety of techniques, including needlepoint, intricate cross-stitch, and colourful and elaborate patchwork and quilting. The abundance of ladies' periodicals published at that time provided inspiration and patterns for fashionable fancy work such as needlecases, pin cushions and sewing caskets. Ladies' workboxes, much collected to this day, were packed with all the essential tools of an accomplished needlewoman. This quilt, criss-crossed with chequered ribbons and studded with pretty pearly buttons, makes a stylish cover for a sewing basket.

1 *Place the polyester wadding between the silk top and satin brocade back of the quilt. Lightly tack the pieces together.*

2 *Cut the pink ribbon into lengths and lay them across the quilt in an even lattice pattern. Pin and then tack them in place. Hand or machine stitch along each side of the ribbon.*

3 *Sew the iridescent plastic buttons to mark each crossing of the ribbons and sew a larger pearl button in the centre of each square.*

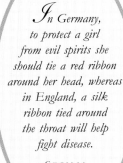

In Germany, to protect a girl from evil spirits she should tie a red ribbon around her head, whereas in England, a silk ribbon tied around the throat will help fight disease.

CECILIA
CAVENDISH

MATERIALS

Lightweight polyester wadding 45 × 35 cm (18 × 14 in)

Grey silk 45 × 35 cm (18 × 14 in)

Grey satin brocade 45 × 35 cm (18 × 14 in)

Needle

Thread to match ribbons and background

3.5 m (11 ft) of bobble-edged pink chequered ribbon 2.5 cm (1 in) wide

12 iridescent flecked plastic buttons, 1.5 cm (1/2 in) in diameter

20 mother-of-pearl buttons, 2 cm (3/4 in) in diameter

2 m (6 1/2 ft) of dark pink and black bobble-edged chequered ribbon 3.5 cm (1 1/2 in) wide

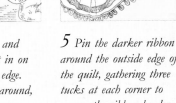

4 *Tuck the top and back of the quilt in on itself around the edge. Hand stitch all around, making a neat seam.*

5 *Pin the darker ribbon around the outside edge of the quilt, gathering three tucks at each corner to ensure the ribbon border lies flat. Sew on neatly with black thread, turning the ends over to make a hidden join.*

GLASS PLATE

*D*ÉCOUPAGE practitioners were eager to try all sorts of inventive techniques. You can still find occasional examples of Victorian glass plates that have been découpaged from behind the glass. In fact, the whole technique is back to front: the glue is applied to the front of the paper motif, paint is applied behind the paper and all this shows through on a brilliant smooth glass surface.

'Tis the last rose of summer
Left blooming alone;
All her lovely companions
Are faded and gone;
No flower of her kindred,
No rose-bud is nigh,
To reflect back her blushes,
Or give sigh for sigh …

Irish Melodies 1821
THOMAS MOORE 1779–1852

MATERIALS

Shaped glass plate

Victorian Valentine scraps

Small scissors

PVA glue, diluted with water

Brush for glue

Pink paint

Paintbrush

Polyurethane varnish

Brush for varnish

SONG

Her cheeks are like roses
Her eyes they are blue
And her beauty is mine
If her heart it is true

Her cheeks are like roses
And though she's away
I shall see her sweet beauty
On some other day

JOHN CLARE 1793–1864

1 Carefully cut out 7 Victorian Valentine scraps. Make sure they are the appropriate shape and size to fit your plate.

2 Apply the diluted PVA glue to the front of your scrap, then press it firmly into place on the back of the plate, taking care to smooth out any trapped air bubbles with your fingers. Allow the PVA glue to dry.

3 Paint the back of the plate, covering the paper scraps with the pink paint. You will need to apply at least 2 coats. Allow to dry thoroughly.

4 Apply 3 coats of varnish over the paint to protect the surface from scuffing and scratches.

*O*nly bring this plate to the table on special occasions. It is not possible to immerse it in water, just sponge it clean and dry with a cloth. You may prefer not to use it at all but to hang it decoratively from the wall with proper plate hangers.

INDEX

A C K N O W L E D G E M E N T S

The author would like to give very special
thanks to Heini Schneebeli for his care and
attention to detail in taking the really lovely
photographs in this book. And to all my good
friends who have happily lent me beautiful objects
from their own homes: Raynes Minns, Duffy Ayers,
Anthea Sieveking, Alan Stewart, Sophie Hedworth,
Marion Manheimer, Pat Schleger, Gloria Nichol,
Dulcie Beilin Morel. Special thanks to Anna
Bentinck for invaluable help with finding the
original Victorian material; to Mamelok Press Ltd,
Bury St Edmunds, IP32 6NJ, for supplying the
Victorian scraps throughout the book; and to
V. V. Rouleaux, Ribbon Supplies, 10 Symons Street,
London, SW3 2TJ (0171-730 3125).
The engravings for the book plate on pages 14–15
were photocopied from copyright-free source
books published by Dover Publications.

Very special thanks to my two children,
Hannah and Raphael, and to Teo Spurring, who
have been so patient, understanding and supportive
during the production of this book.